Junior School Library
1639 Yonge Street
Toronto, Ontario
M4T 2W6
www.yorkschool.com

12 REASONS TO LOVE
BASKETBALL

by Phil Ervin

www.12StoryLibrary.com

Copyright © 2018 by 12-Story Library, Mankato, MN 56003. All rights reserved. No part of this book may be reproduced or utilized in any form or by any means without written permission from the publisher.

12-Story Library is an imprint of Bookstaves and Press Room Editions

Produced for 12-Story Library by Red Line Editorial

Photographs ©: Ronald Martinez/Pool Photo/AP Images, cover, 1; JoffreyM/Shutterstock Images, 4; Art Babych/Shutterstock Images, 5; Sergey Novikov/Shutterstock Images, 6; Ververidis Vasilis/Shutterstock Images, 7; Karl DeBlaker/AP Images, 8; A. Ricardo/Shutterstock Images, 9; Paul Vathis/AP Images, 10; Zach Bolinger/Icon Sportswire/AP Images, 11; Rawpixel.com/Shutterstock Images, 12; bikeriderlondon/Shutterstock Images, 13; Chuck Myers/Cal Sport Media/AP Images, 15; AP Images, 16, 29; Rob Carr/AP Images, 17; Jim Mone/AP Images, 18; Anthony Nesmith/Cal Sport Media/AP Images, 19, 28; Michael Conroy/Darron Cummings/AP Images, 20; XiXinXing/Shutterstock Images, 22; Erika Cross/Shutterstock Images, 23; CP DC Press/Shutterstock Images, 24; Elise Amendola/AP Images, 25; Charlie Neibergall/AP Images, 26; Kenneth Sponsler/Shutterstock Images, 27

Library of Congress Cataloging-in-Publication Data
Names: Ervin, Phil, author.
Title: 12 reasons to love basketball / by Phil Ervin.
Other titles: Twelve reasons to love basketball
Description: Mankato, Minnesota : 12 Story Library, 2018. | Series: Sports report | Includes bibliographical references and index. | Audience: Grade 4 to 6.
Identifiers: LCCN 2016047115 (print) | LCCN 2016053835 (ebook) | ISBN 9781632354266 (hardcover : alk. paper) | ISBN 9781632354952 (pbk. : alk. paper) | ISBN 9781621435471 (hosted e-book)
Subjects: LCSH: Basketball--Juvenile literature.
Classification: LCC GV885.1 .E13 2018 (print) | LCC GV885.1 (ebook) | DDC 796.323--dc23
LC record available at https://lccn.loc.gov/2016047115

Printed in China
022017

Access free, up-to-date content on this topic plus a full digital version of this book. Scan the QR code on page 31 or use your school's login at 12StoryLibrary.com.

Table of Contents

All You Need Is a Ball and a Hoop 4

Almost Anyone Can Play 6

Superstars Change the Game 8

Basketball's Records Are Hard to Beat 10

There's Skill and Strategy 12

You Can Expect the Unexpected 14

Great Coaches Are Leaders 16

The Future Is Bright 18

March Madness Is Magical 20

Basketball Can Be Played Inside or Out 22

Basketball Is Worldwide 24

Towns Love Their Basketball Teams 26

Fact Sheet 28

Glossary 30

For More Information 31

Index 32

About the Author 32

All You Need Is a Ball and a Hoop

One of the best things about basketball is that it doesn't require fancy equipment. All players need is a ball and a hoop. They don't need helmets, pads, gloves, sticks, or bats.

It all started in 1891. This is when Dr. James Naismith invented basketball. Naismith was from Canada. He was teaching in Massachusetts. He wanted to create an indoor sport his students could play in winter. He first used peach baskets and soccer balls as equipment. It was a game of skill, not strength. The new sport gained a lot of attention. In two years, basketball had spread around the world.

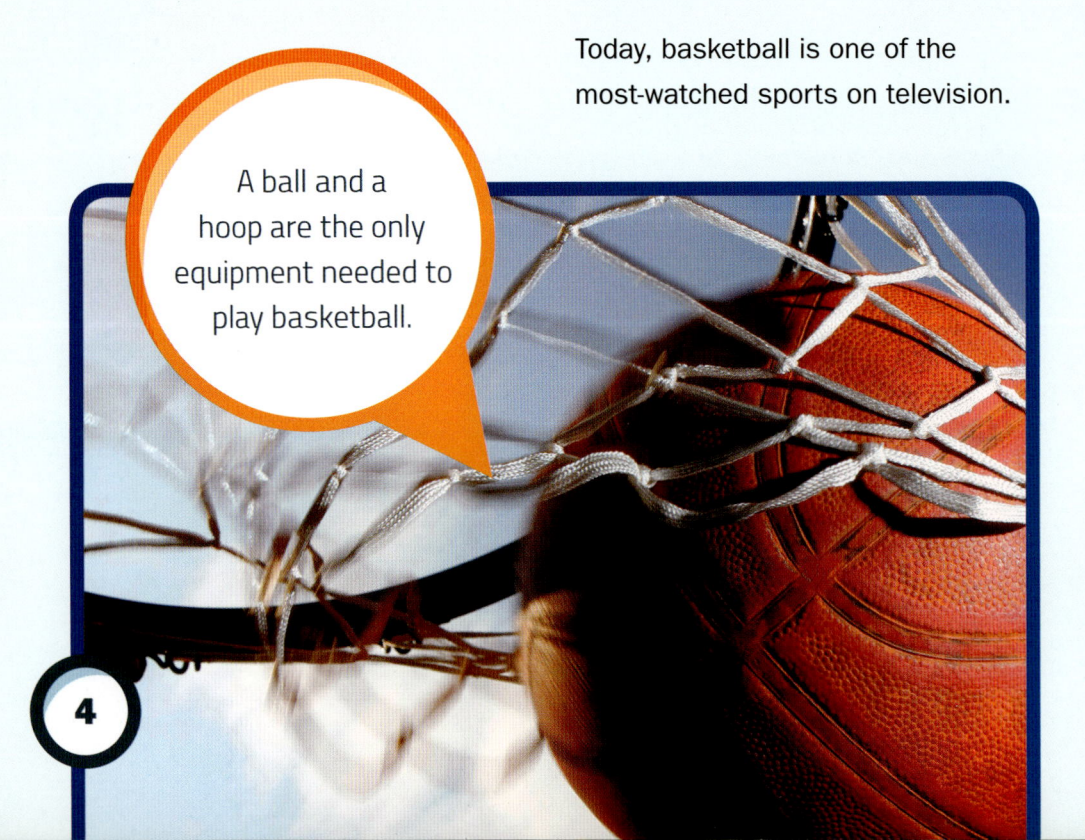

Today, basketball is one of the most-watched sports on television.

A ball and a hoop are the only equipment needed to play basketball.

700
Number of Division I men's and women's basketball teams in the NCAA.

- Basketball is a game for nearly everyone.
- James Naismith invented basketball in 1891.
- The game's greatest players play in the NBA and WNBA.

"NAISMITH-BALL"

Though he invented basketball, Naismith didn't like to brag. His students suggested he name the new sport "Naismith-ball." Instead, he called it "basket ball" because of the peach baskets. The name later became basketball, as one word.

The best players are in the National Basketball Association (NBA) and the Women's National Basketball Association (WNBA). College basketball is also very popular. The National Collegiate Athletic Association (NCAA) tournament is nicknamed March Madness.

But what makes basketball great is that just about everyone can enjoy it. Fans can cheer on many different college and professional teams. People can play in their neighborhoods and schools. Basketball brings people together. It teaches them how to work as a team. And all it takes is a ball and a hoop.

James Naismith is remembered as the Father of Basketball.

Almost Anyone Can Play

Almost anyone can play basketball—young and old, male and female. It's fun for everyone.

Basketball has different options for different levels. Some people play in pickup games. Those are for players who just want to have fun. Competitive leagues are more serious about winning. Some people like playing with a full team. Each team has five players on the court at all times. It's called five-on-five basketball. Other people like playing three-on-three or one-on-one.

There are different ways to play the sport. In the game 21, players aren't on teams. It's like one-on-one. The first player to score 21 points wins. In H-O-R-S-E, players try to make the same shots as their opponents. Lightning is a free-throw contest

Basketball is a sport people of any age can enjoy.

with a twist. Players line up and try to make a shot before the person behind them does.

Youth leagues start at very young ages. Some children learn the basics of the sport as preschoolers. Many older men and women play in pickup leagues. The National Senior Games even feature a tournament for people 85 and older.

The sport is almost as popular with girls as with boys. In 2015, nearly a million students played high school basketball. Of those, 44 percent were girls.

People with disabilities can also play basketball. A professional wheelchair basketball league began in 2017.

Wheelchair basketball is also an event in the Paralympics. In 2016, Team USA won gold for both the men's and women's events.

> Wheelchair basketball adapts the sport so people with disabilities can play.

22
Total number of men's and women's teams playing wheelchair basketball at the 2016 Paralympics.

- Basketball is a sport for people of all ages and skill levels.
- There are many ways to play the game.
- Wheelchair basketball is a Paralympic event.

3

Superstars Change the Game

Over the years, some NBA players have become superstars. Many people believe Michael Jordan is the greatest player of all time. He led the Chicago Bulls to six NBA championships. He also won five league Most Valuable Player (MVP) awards.

LeBron James is close behind Jordan as the best of the best. As of 2016, James has won three championships with the Cleveland Cavaliers and the Miami Heat. He has also won four NBA MVP awards.

Stephen Curry of the Golden State Warriors competed against James in big games. In 2015, Curry led the Warriors to a championship. They beat James's Cavaliers. A year later, the Cavaliers beat Golden State in the Finals. Curry holds the record for most three-pointers in a season.

> Michael Jordan may just be the best to ever play basketball.

STARS OF YESTERDAY

The stars of today look up to the stars of years past. Kareem Abdul-Jabbar and Magic Johnson won many titles with the Lakers. Boston's Larry Bird and Houston's Hakeem Olajuwon also helped make the sport what it is today.

Two NBA MVPs retired in 2016. Kobe Bryant retired from the Los Angeles Lakers. San Antonio Spurs star Tim Duncan also ended his NBA career.

> LeBron James is the biggest superstar in the NBA today.

20
Seasons Kobe Bryant played in the NBA with the Los Angeles Lakers.

- Many people think Michael Jordan is the best player ever.
- LeBron James may be the greatest player still in the NBA.
- Many of the top WNBA players played at UConn.

The WNBA is full of superstars, too. Tina Charles leads the New York Liberty. Diana Taurasi plays for the Phoenix Mercury. And Maya Moore is with the Minnesota Lynx. All three stars came from the University of Connecticut (UConn). It is known as the top women's college team.

4

Basketball's Records Are Hard to Beat

On March 2, 1962, Hall of Famer Wilt Chamberlain made basketball history. He scored 100 points in a game. His Philadelphia Warriors beat the New York Knicks 169–147. It was an amazing performance. Chamberlain played in many record-breaking games. Of the 10 highest single-game point totals, 6 belong to him. He holds 72 NBA records in all.

As of 2016, no one has beat Chamberlain's 100-point record. Kobe Bryant came the closest. In 2006, Bryant scored 81 points in a game. His Los Angeles Lakers beat the Toronto Raptors 122–104.

The NBA isn't the only place where records are set. Jack Taylor of Grinnell College scored 138 points in a 2012 game. This broke the NCAA single-game points record. In 2013, the Kentucky women's

Wilt Chamberlain celebrates his 100-point game.

17
Record number of NBA championships for the Boston Celtics.

- Wilt Chamberlain holds the record for points in a game.
- Jack Taylor holds the NCAA points record for a game.
- Player Bill Russell and coaches Phil Jackson and Geno Auriemma each have 11 championships.

All players dream of winning championships. One NBA player set the record for championship titles. Bill Russell won 11 championships with the Boston Celtics. Of those, eight came in a row. Russell led the way as Boston won those eight championships from 1959 to 1966.

Eleven seems to be a magic number for championship records. Phil Jackson won 11 NBA titles as a coach. He coached the Chicago Bulls and Los Angeles Lakers. As of 2016, Geno Auriemma has 11 NCAA championships as a coach. He coaches the UConn women's team.

team beat Baylor 133–130. As of 2016, this was the highest-scoring women's game in NCAA Division I history.

Coach Geno Auriemma (center) leads the UConn women's team.

There's Skill and Strategy

Basketball is a game of skill and strategy. Players and coaches must do their part.

It's a coach's job to put the right players in the right places. Some teams have fast players. Coaches have them run up and down the floor quickly. Other teams have bigger players. Coaches have them play close to the basket. Still other teams have shooters who can make long shots. Coaches have those players take three-pointers. Professional and college teams are making more three-pointers than ever before.

Coaches draw up plays. Players then make them happen on the court. Players must go to certain

Coaches must design plays that fit the team's skills.

other parts of the game don't matter as much.

There's strategy for defense, too. Defense is the part of the game where a team tries to stop the other team from scoring. Some teams use man-to-man defense. That's when each player guards a player from the other team. There's also zone defense. In zone defense, each player defends a certain area of the floor. The best defensive teams use a mix of man-to-man and zone.

> Good strategy means good defense.

spots on the floor. Teammates will throw them the ball so they can take a shot. The other teammates help by getting in the other team's way. This is called setting a pick or screen.

Passing is an important part of the game. It's the best way to move the ball past the other team. Without good passing and teamwork, the

5
Positions in basketball: point guard, shooting guard, small forward, power forward, and center.

- Coaches and players use different strategies.
- Passing is an important part of the game.
- There are two kinds of defense: man-to-man and zone.

13

6

You Can Expect the Unexpected

Sometimes underdog teams beat teams they're not expected to beat. When that happens, it's called an upset.

In 1994, the Denver Nuggets were the eighth seed in the Western Conference playoffs. That means they were the weakest playoff team. The Seattle Supersonics were the first seed. That means they were the best in the conference. But the Nuggets beat the Supersonics three games to two.

Basketball has its share of unexpected comebacks, too. In 2004, the Houston Rockets were losing to San Antonio by 10 points. There was roughly a minute to go. Tracy McGrady then scored 13 points in 33 seconds. The Rockets won 81–80.

Some of basketball's most unexpected moments were slam dunks. To dunk, a player leaps and slams the ball into the basket

QUADRUPLE-DOUBLE

Great players get triple-doubles. That is when a player has a double-digit total in three different areas of play. But four players in NBA history have gotten an unexpected quadruple-double. That's a double-digit total in four areas.

36
Points Utah was down in 1996 before beating Denver in the biggest comeback in NBA history as of 2016.

- Upsets and comebacks happen in basketball.
- Sometimes underdogs beat top teams.
- NBA and WNBA players sometimes make unexpected dunks.

Brittney Griner jumps for a dunk.

with hands above the rim. In many cases, a player must be tall in order to dunk. Yet five-foot-nine Nate Robinson won three NBA Slam Dunk Contests. He won in 2006, 2009, and 2010. In 2002, Lisa Leslie of the Los Angeles Sparks wowed fans with a dunk. She was the first WNBA player to dunk in a game. Today, Brittney Griner of the Phoenix Mercury thrills fans with many dunks.

7

Great Coaches Are Leaders

There have been many great coaches in basketball history. They are teachers but also leaders. A good coach can make a big difference.

From 1964 to 1975, John Wooden led the University of California, Los Angeles (UCLA) to 10 NCAA championships. Seven of those titles came back to back.

Wooden created a coaching style he called the Pyramid of Success. Today, many athletes and teams still follow his system. Even businesses follow it. He taught that success is built piece by piece. Friendship and cooperation are some of the first pieces.

Those lead to things such as team spirit and confidence.

Phil Jackson was one of the best NBA coaches. From 1989 to 2011, he coached the Bulls and Lakers.

Under Coach Wooden (center), UCLA won seven championships in a row.

THINK ABOUT IT

In what ways are coaches like teachers? What coach or teacher has taught you important lessons? What were those lessons?

1,098
Record number of wins for Pat Summitt.

- Basketball coaches are leaders and teachers.
- John Wooden and Phil Jackson are considered some of the best coaches.
- Pat Summitt is perhaps the best coach in NCAA history.

He has more NBA titles than any other coach. He coached great players such as Michael Jordan, Kobe Bryant, and Shaquille O'Neal.

Jackson used a coaching strategy called the triangle offense. It helped his teams win 11 NBA titles. Jackson also taught his players that strong minds are just as important as strong bodies.

Pat Summitt was one of the best college basketball coaches in history. She coached the Tennessee women's team. She retired with more victories than any other NCAA coach in history. As a coach, Summitt asked a lot of her players. Her goal was to turn players into leaders.

Pat Summitt demanded a lot from her players.

8

The Future Is Bright

The Minnesota Timberwolves have some of the NBA's hottest young players. Before the 2014–15 season, the Timberwolves traded for Andrew Wiggins. He became Rookie of the Year. That same year, the Timberwolves drafted Zach LaVine. In his first two seasons, he won the All-Star Dunk Contest. In 2015, the Timberwolves drafted Karl-Anthony Towns. He won Rookie of the Year in 2016. The three may lead the team into the future.

On the women's side, Jewell Loyd, Chiney Ogwumike, and Elena Delle Donne are among the top young players. All three won WNBA Rookie of the Year Awards.

Over the years, the NBA has had different rules about how old players must be to enter the league.

From left to right, Wiggins, Towns, and LaVine may be the Timberwolves' future.

In 1995, rule changes allowed Kevin Garnett to enter straight out of high school. Kobe Bryant did the same in 1996. LeBron James did it in 2003. But in 2006, the rules changed again. Today, rookies must be at least 19 to enter the NBA. At least one basketball season must pass after they finish high school.

The WNBA has its own rules about when players can join. Players must be 22. They must be done playing college basketball. Otherwise, they must leave college early. Loyd was one of a few players who left college early to join the WNBA.

Jewell Loyd was named WNBA Rookie of the Year.

4,328
Total points Towns, Wiggins, and LaVine scored for the Timberwolves in the 2015–16 season.

- The Minnesota Timberwolves have some of the NBA's best young players.
- The future is bright for the WNBA with young players such as Jewell Loyd.
- The NBA and WNBA have rules about players' ages when entering the league.

March Madness Is Magical

Every spring, teams play in the NCAA basketball championship tournaments.

There's a tournament for men's teams and another for women's teams.

March Madness leads to the magical moment when a team is named champion.

UPSET TEAMS

Middle Tennessee State. Florida Gulf Coast. Lehigh. Hampton. Coppin State. Santa Clara. Richmond. What do these schools have in common? They were all 15th-seeded underdogs in the NCAA tournament. And they all went on to beat the 2nd-seeded teams. However, as of 2016, no 16th seed has ever beaten a 1st seed.

0.7
Seconds left on the clock before Charlotte Smith made her buzzer-beating shot to win the championship.

- The NCAA basketball tournament decides the men's and women's champions.
- Fans have fun filling out tournament brackets.
- There have been amazing moments in March Madness history.

The tournaments are called March Madness because they're so unpredictable.

The tournament begins with 64 teams. The teams are grouped into four regions. The teams in each region are then seeded, or ranked. The winners of each game go on to play the next round. Eventually, the tournament gets down to a Sweet Sixteen and Elite Eight. Then there's the Final Four. The last two teams left play in the championship.

Basketball fans enjoy March Madness. Many people try to predict how the tournament might go. They do this by filling out a bracket showing all 64 teams.

Fans also love March Madness for its magical moments. Lorenzo Charles of North Carolina State dunked a teammate's missed three-pointer. This won the 1983 championship. Christian Laettner made a last-second jump shot to put Duke in the 1992 Final Four. In 1994, Charlotte Smith made a buzzer-beating three-pointer. Her shot gave North Carolina its first women's title in history.

10

Basketball Can Be Played Inside or Out

Basketball is popular because it can be played anywhere at any time. Inside or outside. The sport is fun whether it's played in a park or in a famous arena.

In warm weather, many people enjoy basketball outdoors. Many families have hoops in their driveways. Other people play at parks and other public places. These games are often called street basketball. Some of the best street basketball can be found at New York's Rucker Park. Many stars played there. The list includes Kareem Abdul-Jabbar, Nate "Tiny" Archibald, Wilt Chamberlain, and Julius "Dr. J" Erving. Hoop-It-Up features both street basketball and indoor hoops. It's a three-on-three tournament that tours the United States.

Basketball arenas make the game exciting to watch and play indoors. Many basketball courts

Parks are great places for a game of street basketball.

19,830
Number of seats in Madison Square Garden for a basketball game.

- Basketball can be played inside or outdoors.
- Street basketball is played outside in places such as parks.
- Famous basketball arenas are unique.

THINK ABOUT IT

What do you like best—playing basketball indoors or out? Why? Also, what do you like best—watching basketball indoors or out? Why?

are 94 feet (28.6 m) by 50 feet (15.2 m). With small courts, arenas have to be just the right size. They must be large enough to fit many fans but small enough to keep them close to the game.

Many arenas are famous. The New York Knicks and New York Liberty play their home games at Madison Square Garden. The Celtics play at the famed TD Garden.

College basketball arenas have their own history. Duke's Cameron Indoor Stadium and North Carolina's Dean E. Smith Center are special to fans.

Madison Square Garden is home to the Knicks and Liberty.

11

Basketball Is Worldwide

The United States isn't the only country where kids grow up shooting hoops. Basketball's global popularity is on the rise. More and more people around the world play and watch the sport.

The NBA has a strong presence in Europe, China, and India. The league plays preseason games and some regular-season games in other countries.

Games can be viewed in 215 countries and territories and heard in 47 different languages.

In the 2015–16 season, 100 NBA players were from outside the United States. Some of the game's biggest stars have come from other countries. This includes Hall of Famers Hakeem Olajuwon from Nigeria and Yao Ming from China.

The International Basketball Federation (FIBA) manages and

The Olympics features basketball talent from around the world.

OLYMPIANS

Many basketball stars go head to head in the Olympics. In the 2016 Olympics, 26 WNBA players from 9 countries competed. On the men's side, 47 NBA players played for 10 different countries.

promotes basketball worldwide. It organizes many international tournaments. Every four years, teams compete in the FIBA Basketball World Cup and FIBA Women's Basketball World Cup. The US team won both cups in 2014.

450 million
Basketball players and fans in the world, according to FIBA.

- More and more people around the world play and watch basketball.
- Players come from all over the globe.
- The Summer Olympics show the game's global popularity.

FIBA also oversees the Olympic basketball tournament. The Summer Olympics are the biggest stage for international hoops. The United States usually wins. Both the US men's and women's teams won gold at the 2016 Olympics. It was the women's sixth gold in a row. The men have won three straight golds.

Yao Ming of China had a Hall of Fame career.

Towns Love Their Basketball Teams

Basketball is more than just a sport. It's an important part of many communities. This is true in small towns and big cities. People love their hometown teams. Youth, high school, college, and professional hoops bring people together around the world.

Kinston, North Carolina, has been called Basketball Town. It's a small town with only 20,000 people. But they've built a strong basketball program from youth leagues to high school. Seven players from Kinston have gone on to play in the NBA.

College basketball is also important on many campuses. Excitement can take over a school when the basketball teams play well. Bloomington is the home of the University of Indiana. The entire community roots for the Hoosiers.

Fans rally around their favorite basketball team.

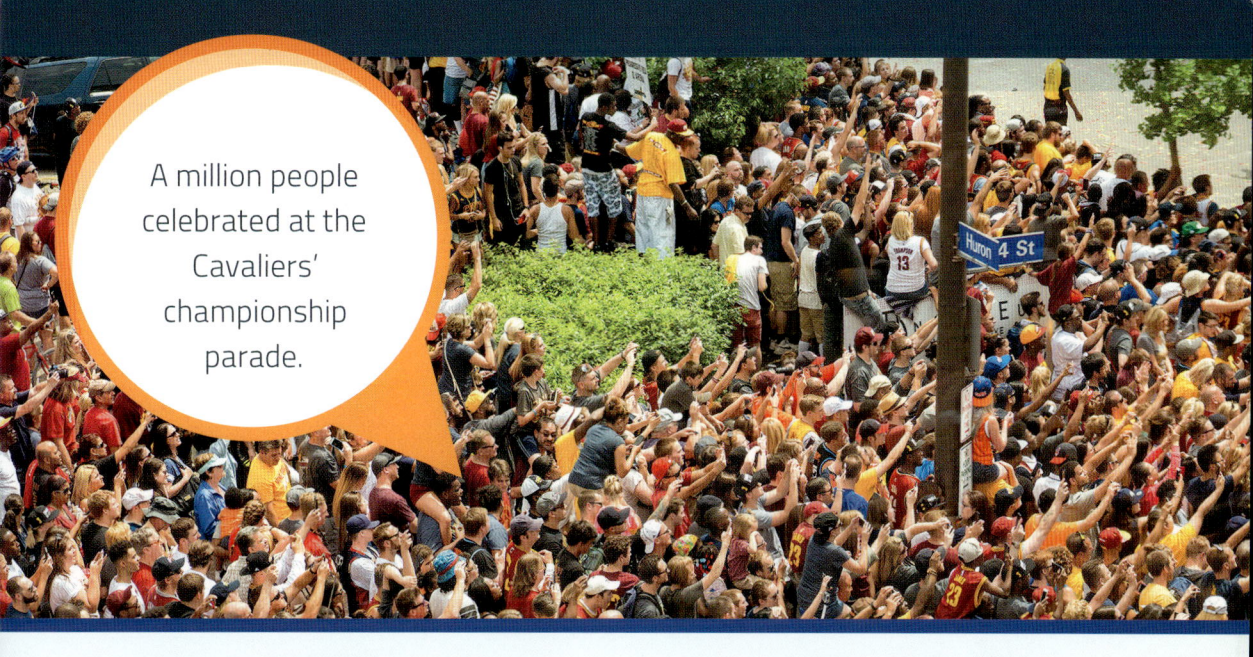

A million people celebrated at the Cavaliers' championship parade.

Cities support their professional teams, too. All of Cleveland, Ohio, seemed to follow the Cavaliers' 2016 championship run. An estimated 1 million people celebrated with the team at the championship parade. It was the city's first major championship in 52 years.

Some cities stick with their teams in good times and in bad. The Chicago Bulls are a team with a history of winning. But the 2016 team wasn't good enough to make the playoffs. Still, the Bulls led the NBA in attendance. They averaged nearly 22,000 fans for each home game.

31 million
Number of likes on the NBA's Facebook page.

- Communities love their basketball teams.
- Cleveland cheered the Cavaliers in the 2016 NBA championship.
- Chicago was highest in attendance, even though the Bulls didn't have a great season.

THINK ABOUT IT

What is your favorite basketball team? Why are they your favorite? Do other people in your community root for them? How does your community support basketball?

Fact Sheet

- A standard basketball court has two baskets. Each basket has a lane, a free-throw line, and a three-point line. Shots made inside the three-point line are worth two points. Baskets made from behind it are worth three points.

- The NBA has 30 teams. The league is divided into two conferences. Each conference has three divisions of five teams. The top eight teams in each conference go to the NBA Playoffs.

- The WNBA is divided into two six-team conferences. The league's top eight teams reach the postseason.

- There are 351 NCAA Division I men's basketball teams. There are 349 Division I women's teams. There are also teams at the Division II and Division III levels.

- In 1977, long before the WNBA formed, the New Orleans Jazz drafted Lusia Harris-Stewart of Delta State University. She decided not to try out for the team. Many consider her the greatest center in women's basketball.

Glossary

campus
The grounds of a college or university.

comeback
When a team falls behind in a game or series, then comes back and wins.

disability
An illness or injury that limits physical or mental abilities.

hall of fame
A select group of players considered the best to ever play the game.

league
A collection of teams that compete against one another.

Paralympics
A form of Olympic games for athletes with disabilities.

pickup
In sports, a type of game played just for fun.

preseason
The period before the regular season begins; teams train and play practice games.

strategy
A careful plan or method.

tournament
A competition where teams who lose get knocked out.

underdog
The team not expected to win.

upset
When the team favored to win loses to the underdog team.

For More Information

Books

Frisch, Nate. *The Story of the Golden State Warriors*. Mankato, MN: Creative Education, 2015.

Norwich, Grace. *I Am LeBron James*. New York: Scholastic Paperbacks, 2014.

Silverman, Drew. *Best Sport Ever: Basketball*. Minneapolis, MN: Abdo, 2012.

Williams, Doug. *Great Moments in Olympic Basketball*. Minneapolis, MN: Abdo, 2015.

Visit 12StoryLibrary.com

Scan the code or use your school's login at **12StoryLibrary.com** for recent updates about this topic and a full digital version of this book. Enjoy free access to:

- Digital ebook
- Breaking news updates
- Live content feeds
- Videos, interactive maps, and graphics
- Additional web resources

Note to educators: Visit 12StoryLibrary.com/register to sign up for free premium website access. Enjoy live content plus a full digital version of every 12-Story Library book you own for every student at your school.

Index

Auriemma, Geno, 11

Bryant, Kobe, 9, 10, 17, 19

Chamberlain, Wilt, 10, 22

Charles, Tina, 9

Curry, Stephen, 8

Delle Donne, Elena, 18

Griner, Brittney, 15

International Basketball Federation (FIBA), 24–25

Jackson, Phil, 11, 16–17
James, LeBron, 8, 9, 19
Jordan, Michael, 8, 9, 17

LaVine, Zach, 18
Loyd, Jewell, 18, 19

March Madness, 5, 20–21
Moore, Maya, 9

Naismith, James, 4–5
National Basketball Association (NBA), 5, 8, 9, 10, 11, 14, 15, 16, 17, 18, 19, 24, 25, 26, 27
National Collegiate Athletic Association (NCAA), 5, 10, 11, 16, 17, 20–21

Ogwumike, Chiney, 18
Olympics, 25

Russell, Bill, 11

street basketball, 22
Summit, Pat, 17

Taurasi, Diana, 9
Towns, Karl-Anthony, 18

wheelchair basketball, 7
Wiggins, Andrew, 18
Women's National Basketball Association (WNBA), 5, 9, 14, 15, 18, 19, 25
Wooden, John, 16

Yao Ming, 24

About the Author
Phil Ervin was born and raised in Omaha, Nebraska. He has written five other children's sports books. Phil has worked as a reporter for Fox Sports and the Minnesota Wild.

READ MORE FROM 12-STORY LIBRARY
Every 12-Story Library book is available in many formats. For more information, visit 12StoryLibrary.com.